# Antoni van Leeuwenhoek

## First to See Microscopic Life

# GREAT MINDS OF SCIENCE

# Antoni van Leeuwenhoek
## First to See Microscopic Life

Lisa Yount

**Enslow Publishers, Inc.**

44 Fadem Road          PO Box 38
Box 699                Aldershot
Springfield, NJ 07081  Hants GU12 6BP
USA                    UK

*To all young people who are "curious to know" about*
*nature and all those who teach them*

**Library of Congress Cataloging-in-Publication Data**

Yount, Lisa.
    Antoni van Leeuwenhoek : first to see microscopic life / by Lisa Yount.
      p. cm. — (Great minds of science)
    Includes bibliograpical references (p.   ) and index.
    Summary: A biography of the cloth merchant-turned-scientist who
made many discoveries examining microscopic life.
    ISBN 0-89490-680-1
    1. Leeuwenhoek, Antoni van, 1632–1723—Juvenile literature. 2. Biolo-
gists—Netherlands—Biography. 3. Microscopes—History—
Juvenile literature. [1. Leeuwenhoek, Antoni van, 1632–1723.
2. Biologists. 3. Microscopes. 4. Microscopy.] I. Title. II. Series.
QH31.L55Y68 1996
578'.092—dc20                          96-6057
[B]                                      CIP
                                           AC

Printed in the United States of America

10 9 8 7 6 5 4 3

# Contents

# Introduction: Exploring Hidden Worlds

IN A HOSPITAL, A BABY LIES CRYING. IT IS sick, but no one knows why. A nurse takes a sample of its blood. She sends it to a laboratory in another part of the hospital.

A lab worker smears a bit of the blood on a glass slide. He puts the slide under a microscope. The microscope makes things look hundreds of times bigger than they really are.

Using the microscope, the worker can see the disk-shaped cells that make the baby's blood red. He can also see tiny living things among the cells. They are bacteria. They are making the baby sick. The worker will report the bacteria to the baby's doctor. Then the doctor can prescribe drugs to kill the harmful germs.

In another part of the city, a husband and wife are unhappy. They want a baby but cannot have one. They do not know what is wrong.

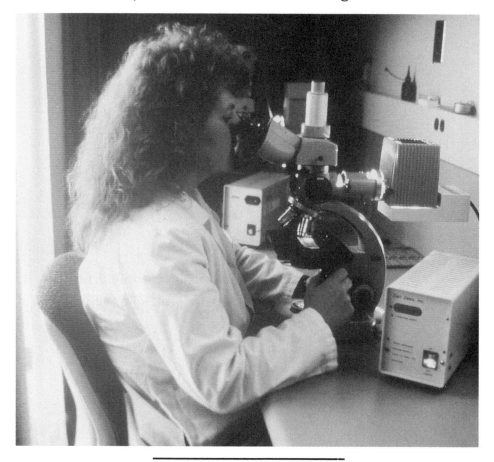

*Scientists use microscopes to learn about nature and protect human health. Antoni van Leeuwenhoek was one of the first to explore the hidden worlds that a microscope reveals.*

A worker in a different laboratory helps them find out. She, too, uses a microscope. She looks at semen, a fluid from the man's body. In it she sees thousands of wiggling things that look like tiny tadpoles. They are sperm cells. The man's body makes these cells.

If the couple is to have a baby, a sperm cell from the man must join with an egg cell from the woman. The worker with the microscope can tell whether the man's sperm cells are healthy. If they are not, treatments may make them so. If they are, doctors will turn their attention to the woman. Either way, the microscope brings the couple closer to their goal.

Many people have better health because of what is learned through a microscope. This device shows things too small to see with the eye alone. A man named Antoni van Leeuwenhoek (an-TON-ee van LAY-wen-hook) was the first to describe many such things in nature. He lived in Holland about three hundred years ago. Holland is also called the Netherlands.

Leeuwenhoek did not invent the microscope.

*Antoni van Leeuwenhoek was the first to see red blood cells, sperm cells, and bacteria through a microscope.*

He was not even the first to use it, but he explored more with it than anyone else of his time or in the hundred years after he died. He was the first to see red blood cells. He was the first to see bacteria. He was the first to see sperm cells and realize what they were. Using microscopes he made himself, he mapped an exciting world that few had dreamed existed.

# A Seller of Cloth

SOME PARTS OF THE DUTCH CITY OF Delft have changed little in hundreds of years. You can still see the town hall, the Old Church, and the New Church. These stone buildings were already old when Antoni van Leeuwenhoek was born in Delft on October 24, 1632.

In those days, Delft was the third biggest city in Holland. One visitor described the town as "very clean, well built, and . . . pleasant."[1] Another said it was the prettiest place he saw in the whole country.

Delft is built on a flat plain or meadow. Like much of Holland, it is below sea level. It would be under water if walls did not keep the sea out.

*The Old Church in Delft was more than three hundred years old
when Antoni van Leeuwenhoek was born. Leeuwenhoek, who
lived in Delft almost all his life, is buried in the church.*

Canals, bordered by lime and poplar trees, ran through the city. The oldest one had been dug around the year 1100. They carried as much traffic as Delft's wide streets. In fact, the town was named for them. The Dutch word *delf* or *delft* means "canal."

When Antoni was born, Holland was fighting for its freedom from Spain. Even so, it was a thriving country, famous for its merchants and craftspeople. It controlled much of the trade inside Europe. It had just begun to trade with the Far East as well.

Delft was thriving, too. Trading ships filled its harbor. Its craftspeople made many kinds of goods. Among the most famous were beautiful china dishes. Antoni's father, Philip, made baskets that may have been used to pack them in. Delft was also famous for its beer. Antoni's mother, Margaretha, came from a family of beer brewers. Their name was van den Berch.

The Leeuwenhoek family lived in a corner house on a small street called Leeuwenport. Their name probably came from this house. *Leeuw* means "lion." (The street's name means "lion gate.") *Hoek* means "corner." So the name meant "the family who lives on the corner of Lion (gate) Street."

Antoni's father died in 1638. Antoni was just five then. Philip didn't leave his family much money. Margaretha had a hard time taking care of Antoni and his four sisters. (Their names were Margriete, Geertruyt, Neeltge, and Catharina. In English they would have been Margie, Gertrude, Nellie, and Catherine.) She married again two years later. Her new husband was a painter named Jacob Molijn.

Jacob had also been married before. He had three children of his own. The couple's new home must have been crowded. Perhaps for that reason, Antoni was sent away to school at this time.

The school was at Warmond, a town about twenty miles from Delft. For a while, Antoni probably lived at his teacher's house. Other pupils lived there, too. Later he stayed with an uncle. The uncle was a law officer in a nearby town.

Antoni's schooling was simple. He learned to

read, write, and do some math. He was not taught any foreign languages, though. No one expected him to need them.

In 1648, Antoni went to Amsterdam to learn a trade. He was sixteen years old. Then, as now, this big city was Holland's capital. It must have been quite a change from quiet Delft.

Antoni worked in a shop that sold cloth, buttons, and other sewing supplies. He seems to have learned the cloth-sellers' trade quickly. One report says that after just six weeks, he passed a mastery exam. Most people took this exam after three years of training.

Antoni soon became the shop's accountant and cashier. That meant he must have been good at math. It also meant his employer trusted him.

The big city did not appeal to Antoni van Leeuwenhoek, though. Delft was his home, and he returned there in 1654 and set up his own cloth store. He married a local woman, Barbara de Mei, on July 29. He may have met her through his work. Her father also sold cloth.

Leeuwenhoek bought a house for himself and

his new bride. Houses had names in those days. Leeuwenhoek called his "The Golden Head." He lived there for the rest of his life.

Leeuwenhoek's new life started with a bang—one that nearly wrecked the city. In the same year he came back to Delft, the town's gunpowder storehouse exploded. (The powder was kept to protect the town.) A week later, a visitor reported, "It is a sad sight, whole streets quite razed [flattened]; not one stone upon another. . . . There is scarce [hardly] any house in the town . . . [on which] the [roof] tiles are [not] off."[2]

The people of Delft soon repaired the damage, though. Lives went back to their normal patterns. Leeuwenhoek went on selling wool, linen, and silk to the townspeople. They could buy ribbons, lace, and buttons in his shop, too. He may have sold some pieces of finished clothing as well.

Leeuwenhoek had to make sure the cloth he sold was of good quality. He used a magnifying glass to do this. The glass made things look only a few times larger than they were. It was good enough, though, to show if the threads in the cloth were straight and tightly woven. Perhaps it also made Leeuwenhoek start thinking about the world of the very small.

People in places like Delft often did city jobs as well as their regular work. Leeuwenhoek earned some of his money this way. The kinds of jobs he held showed that he was a respected man in Delft.

Leeuwenhoek's first job was acting as chamberlain for the sheriffs of Delft. He began this work on January 24, 1660. The sheriffs were the town's chief law officers. They met in a big room in the town hall. Leeuwenhoek's job was to keep that room clean.

When the sheriffs had a meeting, Leeuwenhoek had to set up a fire in the fireplace. He made sure the fire was safely put out after the meeting was over. He put out the candles that had lit the room, too. If any unburned coals were left in the fireplace, he could keep and sell them; his job contract said so. The contract also made him

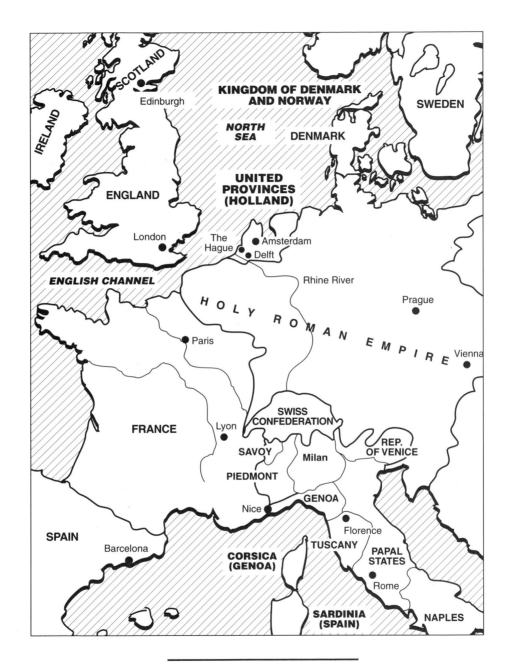

IRELAND

SCOTLAND
Edinburgh

KINGDOM OF DENMARK
AND NORWAY

SWEDEN

NORTH
SEA
DENMARK

ENGLAND

UNITED
PROVINCES
(HOLLAND)

London

The
Hague

Amsterdam
Delft

ENGLISH CHANNEL

Rhine River

HOLY  ROMAN  EMPIRE

Prague

Paris

Vienna

FRANCE

Lyon

SWISS
CONFEDERATION

SAVOY

Milan

REP.
OF VENICE

PIEDMONT

GENOA

SPAIN

Nice

Barcelona

CORSICA
(GENOA)

Florence

TUSCANY

PAPAL
STATES

Rome

SARDINIA
(SPAIN)

NAPLES

*When Antoni was born, Holland, or the United Provinces, was in rebellion against Spain. The Dutch won their independence from Spain in 1648. Holland quickly became a world power.*

promise to "keep to himself whatever he may overhear in the chamber."[3]

In other words, Leeuwenhoek was a kind of janitor. Chances are, though, that he did not spend much time scrubbing town hall floors. Most likely he hired others to do that.

Later Leeuwenhoek did other town jobs as well. In 1669, for instance, he became a surveyor. He had to pass a hard math test to get this post. His job was to measure plots of land that were going to be sold.

Ten years later, Leeuwenhoek took on the job of wine gauger. He tested the purity of wines sold in Delft. He also checked the size of the vessels the wines were sold in. As both surveyor and wine gauger, Leeuwenhoek had to measure very precisely. That suited him well. He was always a careful observer. He used measurement a lot in his science work, too.

Leeuwenhoek's life was quiet, but it was not always happy. He and Barbara Leeuwenhoek had five children, but four died as babies. Many families had such losses in those days. The only child who grew up was a daughter, Maria, born in 1656. Leeuwenhoek's mother died in 1664. Two years later, Barbara Leeuwenhoek died as well.

Leeuwenhoek married again on January 25, 1671. His new wife was named Cornelia Swalmius. She came from an educated family. Her father was a minister. Her brother was a doctor. Leeuwenhoek may have learned some science from them. Most likely, though, his thoughts had already turned toward science several years before.

In 1667 or 1668, Leeuwenhoek did something new. He visited another country—England. No one knows just why he went.

England and Holland had been at war, but the war was dying down at this time. It would flare up again, off and on, during much of Leeuwenhoek's life. But, as one observer wrote, "the nations . . . [were] at war without being angry."[4] The war was mostly a matter of politics. The Dutch and English people did not dislike each other.

As was true all his life, Leeuwenhoek was curious about all he saw on this trip. As his boat sailed up the Thames River toward London, he passed shining cliffs of chalk. Why, he wondered, were the rocks so white?

After Leeuwenhoek landed, he scraped off a bit of the chalk. He wanted to study it more closely. He broke the chalk particles apart. To his surprise, he found they were not white at all. They were clear or transparent, like glass, but when they were all together, they somehow added up to white.

While in London, Leeuwenhoek most likely stayed with other people in the cloth trade. Like him, they would have been used to peering through magnifying glasses. Like most other educated Londoners, they were probably talking about a man who had done much more than that.

He was an Englishman named Robert Hooke. He had used a microscope to look at different kinds of cloth. He learned more about their structure than cloth merchants had ever seen. He had also looked at mold, cork, and much more.

The microscope showed Hooke things that no one had dreamed existed. He reported that the

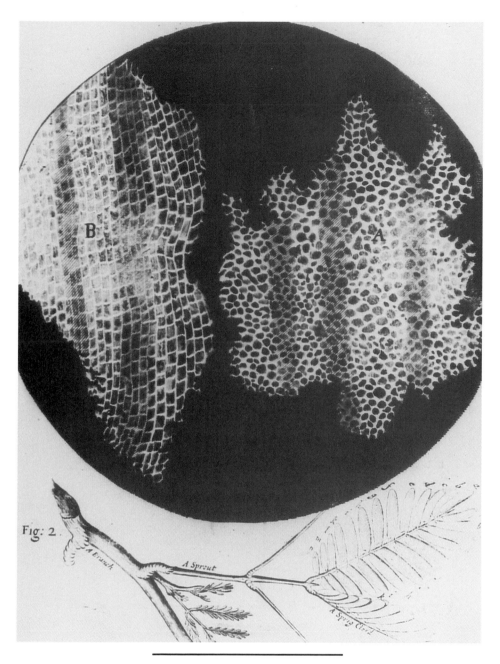

Fig: 2.

These walled chambers in cork, seen under a microscope, reminded Robert Hooke of the cells in which monks lived. Hooke's Micrographia may have inspired Leeuwenhoek to start making and using microscopes.

cork, for instance, was made of tiny, walled spaces. He said they looked like little boxes. They reminded him of the small, bare rooms, called cells, that monks lived in, so he called them cells. This term is still used for the units of which living bodies are made. (Cork is made from tree bark. What Hooke saw was just the tough walls left where the cells of the tree had been.)

Hooke made drawings and descriptions of what he had seen. They were published in a book called *Micrographia*. A new printing of this book appeared just before Leeuwenhoek came to England. For its time, it was a best seller.

Leeuwenhoek could not have read it; he read only Dutch. Other people probably told him what it said, though, and he could see the drawings for himself. Leeuwenhoek may have decided to start making microscopes after seeing *Micrographia*.

Soon after Leeuwenhoek returned to Holland, he began going to weekly meetings held by a group of doctors in Delft. In these meetings, one doctor cut up a dead body while others watched.

The doctors did this to learn more about anatomy, which is the structure of the body.

At least two doctors at these meetings became Leeuwenhoek's friends. They helped him learn more about science and nature. In 1673, one of them changed his life.

# A Most
# Ingenious Person

ONE DOCTOR WHO WENT TO THE meetings in Delft was named Reinier de Graaf. On April 28, 1673, he sent a letter to the Royal Society of London. This group of top British scientists had been formed eleven years before. Its members met to share their work. Science groups of this kind were becoming popular in Europe.

The society had asked scientists in other parts of Europe to write it with news of their discoveries. De Graaf was one of many who replied. His letter described "a certain most ingenious [clever] person here, named Leeuwenhoek."[1] He said

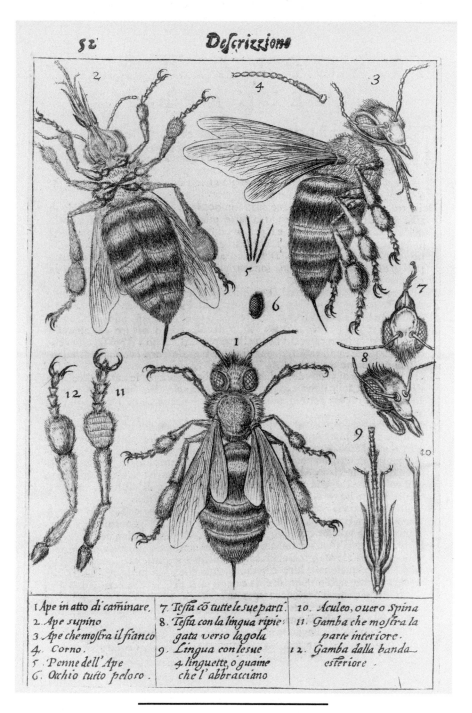

*These pictures of bees, made by Francesco Stelluti in 1630, are the first known drawings made using a microscope.*

Leeuwenhoek was making better microscopes than any that had been seen before.

De Graaf enclosed a letter from Leeuwenhoek. The doctor hoped the society members would like it. De Graaf asked them to write to Leeuwenhoek if they did. Leeuwenhoek, he said, would send more letters if they asked him to.

Leeuwenhoek's letter told about three things he had seen with his microscopes. One was fungus, or mold, such as grows on stale bread. He described the tiny cells that a mold sends out to make new molds. They are called spores. He explained how spores are formed and released. No one had seen single spores before.

Leeuwenhoek also wrote about bees. He described their stingers, eyes, and mouths. His third subject was lice. These small insects live on the skin of people or animals and suck their blood. Robert Hooke also had described molds, bees, and lice in *Micrographia*. Leeuwenhoek corrected three mistakes Hooke had made.

The Royal Society liked Leeuwenhoek's letter. The group asked him to send more. This was the start of an exchange that would last fifty years. During that time, Leeuwenhoek sent the society hundreds of letters.

Leeuwenhoek wrote all his letters in Dutch. He used an old-fashioned form of the language. He even made mistakes in grammar. The Royal Society had to translate the letters into English. (Leeuwenhoek also had to ask friends in Delft to translate their letters to him into Dutch.) Then the group printed them in its journal. Other scientists first learned about Leeuwenhoek by reading these published accounts. Later, groups of his letters were published as books.

Leeuwenhoek's letters were not like most scientists' papers, but more like friendly chats. He jumped from subject to subject, often returning to subjects discussed in earlier letters. The letters contained many details of Leeuwenhoek's daily life, and each detail had a purpose. It told something about how or where an experiment or observation was made. Such facts can be important in science.

Leeuwenhoek's first reply to the Royal Society

*Leeuwenhoek's microscopes look very different from the microscopes of today. This reproduction of a Leeuwenhoek microscope was made in 1887.*

was sent on August 15, 1673. In it he admitted his lack of training in writing and science. "I have no style . . . with which to express my thoughts properly," he wrote. "I have . . . been brought up [trained] . . . only to business."[2] He went on to describe his latest discoveries.

Like most of Leeuwenhoek's later letters, this

one contained drawings. They showed the parts of bees and lice described in his first letter. He explained that he had not made the drawings himself. He couldn't draw well, he said. Instead, he asked artists in Delft to look through his microscopes at things he was writing about. They then drew what they saw. Most of the drawings in his later letters were done the same way.

Leeuwenhoek also measured almost all the things he described. He was much more careful about this than most other scientists of his day. To be sure, some of his units might seem odd. He compared things to a grain of sand or the eye of a louse. He knew just how big each of these was. A large grain of sand, for instance, was 1/30 of an inch.

In his August 15 letter, Leeuwenhoek wrote that all his observations and thoughts came from his own work. The same was true of his microscopes. He made each part of them himself.

No one knows just when or how Leeuwenhoek learned to make microscopes. His first letter says, though, that they were "recently invented." He wrote that he first looked at bees through them "about two years ago."[3] That means he probably started making and using microscopes around 1670 or 1671.

Leeuwenhoek's microscopes were not at all like those used today. For one thing, they were just a few inches long. One could fit in the palm of a person's hand. Also, each had only one lens. A lens is a curved piece of glass or other clear substance that focuses (brings together) rays of light to form an image. In a microscope, it makes things look larger than they are. A microscope with only one lens is called a simple microscope. It is really just a powerful form of magnifying glass.

Most microscopes used today are compound microscopes. They have two or more lenses. One lens is in the eyepiece, which is the part people look into. The other is at the bottom of the microscope's tube or barrel. Most modern microscopes have several bottom lenses set in a sort of wheel. They enlarge things by different amounts; the stronger the lens, the bigger things look. A person chooses which lens to use by turning the wheel.

A lens makes things look larger because it is curved. Light moves in straight lines, called rays, but when the light goes from one substance to another, the rays can be bent. If you put a straight stick part way into the water, the stick will seem to bend at the spot where the water meets the air. This is because light rays move through water more slowly than they move through air. The same thing happens when light from the air goes through glass.

A lens that bulges out, like a bubble, is called convex. If it curves in, like a bowl, it is concave. The direction of the curve affects how the lens bends light, as does the deepness of the curve. These things determine whether the lens will make things seen through it look larger or smaller, and by how much. A convex lens makes things look larger.

Lenses must be shaped very carefully. Round pieces of glass are first ground down with sand or other gritty material. Then they are polished smooth with fine-grained putty.

Lenses that make things look just a little larger can help people see better. An English scientist named Roger Bacon pointed this out in the thirteenth century. People put such lenses in frames so they could be worn. These were the first eyeglasses. They were also, in a way, the first simple microscopes.

Late in the sixteenth century, people found out how to make lenses that enlarged things much more. Some were used in compound microscopes. No one knows for sure who invented such microscopes. They were in use, though, more than thirty years before Leeuwenhoek was born.

Why did Leeuwenhoek use simple microscopes instead of compound ones? Simple ones were easier and cheaper to make, for one thing. At that time, they also could be better. Lenses made then distorted (changed) the shape and color of things seen through them. The larger and stronger the lens, the worse these problems were. Using two lenses made them greater still. A simple microscope could enlarge things more than a compound one without distorting them.

Leeuwenhoek never said just how he made his lenses. All we know is that they were very, very good. They were also very small. Most were the size of a pinhead. Small lenses could be made clearer than large ones. Leeuwenhoek's lenses were also very convex. They were almost, but not quite, round.

An Irish doctor named Thomas Molyneux (MOL-ee-no) came to see Leeuwenhoek in 1685. Molyneux belonged to the Royal Society. The group had asked him to study Leeuwenhoek's microscopes. He wrote that the best ones he was allowed to see "do not magnify much . . . more than several [other] glasses [microscopes] I have seen." But, he noted, "they far surpass them all . . . in their extreme clearness."[4]

Some may have magnified more as well. Leeuwenhoek would not show anyone his best microscopes, but Molyneux said Leeuwenhoek told him that "they performed far beyond any that he had showed me."[5] The best Leeuwenhoek microscope left today enlarges by 266 times; it makes things look 266 times as big as they really are.

The lens in a Leeuwenhoek microscope was set into a hole between two metal plates, most often brass or silver. The plates were joined together with rivets. Leeuwenhoek made his own plates. Sometimes he even purified his own metal from metal-bearing rocks.

Just in front of the lens, a pin stuck out from a platform or stage. This pin held the thing to be looked at. A screw was attached to the platform. It moved the pin closer to or farther from the lens. That brought the object into focus so it could be seen clearly. Another screw raised or lowered the pin. A small wooden handle turned the pin around. In a modern microscope, the lenses rather than the object are moved during focusing.

Today, something to be looked at under a microscope most often is put on a glass slide. Leeuwenhoek didn't have slides. If he wanted to look at a small insect, he just stuck it on the end of the pin. If he wanted to see something larger, he cut a thin slice of it with his shaving razor. He glued this slice to a small glass plate. Sometimes he put the slice between two plates. Then he glued the plate or plates to the pin. If he wanted to look at tiny creatures in water, he put the water in a small glass tube. Then he glued the tube to the pin.

Someone using a microscope today would look down through the microscope's barrel. Leeuwenhoek, instead, held his little microscope close to his eye. He looked through the lens at what was on the pin. In the daytime, he stood near a window. The sun gave him the light he needed. At night, he used the light of a candle.

A German visitor described what looking through a Leeuwenhoek microscope was like. He wrote, "You have to put the side of the microscope, where the lens is, against your forehead. . . . [You] look upwards through the tiny glass [lens]. . . . After some time, [this] would become tiresome."[6] It never seemed to tire Leeuwenhoek, though.

It is easy to take one slide out of a modern microscope and put another in. Leeuwenhoek, though, seldom changed what was on the pin in one of his microscopes. If he wanted to look at something new, he built another microscope. He

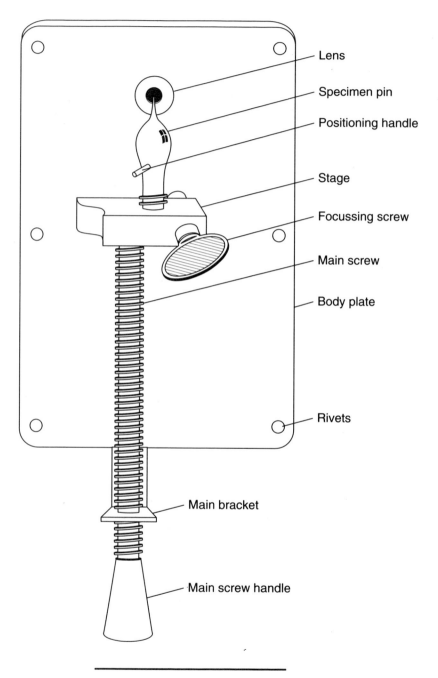

Lens

Specimen pin

Positioning handle

Stage

Focussing screw

Main screw

Body plate

Rivets

Main bracket

Main screw handle

*Leeuwenhoek built all his own microscopes. Most of them had a structure like this.*

made at least 247 during his life. Of these, just nine are left today.

Leeuwenhoek's microscopes were probably better than any others of his time. But Martin Folkes, another Royal Society member, knew they were not the real secret of the Dutchman's success. That, Folkes wrote, was due to Leeuwenhoek's "great judgment and experience in . . . using them." It was also due to the time and care Leeuwenhoek spent on each thing he looked at. He studied it over and over. Because of this, he could "form better judgment of the nature of his objects . . . than it can be imagined any other person can do."[7]

# "Little Animals"

IN THE SUMMER OF 1674, LEEUWENHOEK visited an inland lake called Berkelse. It was about two hours' travel from Delft. He wrote about his trip in a letter to the Royal Society on September 7.

In the summer, Leeuwenhoek said, the water of Berkelse Lake filled with "little green clouds."[1] Local people thought the clouds were made by dew. He himself doubted this. He had wanted to see for himself what the clouds were made of, so he put some of the lake water in a glass tube. Then he looked at it through one of his microscopes.

He saw "earthy particles, and some green streaks."[2] Each streak, he wrote, was about as thick as a human hair. The streaks coiled in spirals, like snakes. Far stranger, though, were

> *many little animals. . . . Some were roundish. . . . Others, a bit bigger, . . . [were] oval [egg-shaped]. On these last I saw two little legs near the head. . . . Two . . . fins [were] at the . . . [rear] end of the body. . . . These animalcules [little animals] had divers [different] colors. Some . . . [were] whitish and transparent [clear]. . . . Others [had] green and glittering . . . scales. . . . The motion of most of these animalcules in the water was so swift, and so various . . . that it was wonderful to see.*[3]

These creatures, Leeuwenhoek said, were about a thousand times smaller than the smallest living thing he had seen so far. That was a tiny, spiderlike mite that lived on cheese. When Leeuwenhoek compared sizes, he spoke of volume, not length. A cheese mite is smaller than the dot at the end of this sentence. A "little animal" was about one tenth as long as a cheese mite.

No one had dreamed that such minute living things existed. They could be seen only through a good microscope. Even Hooke had not found them. Leeuwenhoek would study many kinds of "little animals" during his life. They were his greatest discovery.

Today, most of Leeuwenhoek's "little animals" would be called protists. They are neither plants nor animals. Most have just one cell. There are many kinds of protists. Leeuwenhoek described his animals so well that modern scientists often can tell which kinds he saw.

Two years after his visit to Berkelse Lake, Leeuwenhoek described microscopic life forms, now sometimes called microbes, in much more detail. He had looked for them in water from rain, melted snow, and the sea. He had studied drinking water from his well, too. He saw "little animals" in all of these. The best place to find them, he wrote, was in water in which black pepper had been soaked.

Leeuwenhoek sent his long letter about the animals on October 9, 1676. Part of it was a sort of journal. It told how the numbers and kinds of microbes in water from different sources had changed from day to day.

The first microbes Leeuwenhoek described were in rain water. The water had stayed in a pot for several days. One microbe was a protist now called vorticella. Leeuwenhoek wrote that these creatures

> *sometimes stuck out two little horns. . . . [These] moved after the fashion of a horse's ears. The part between these little horns was flat, their body else being roundish. . . . It ran somewhat to a point at the hind end. . . . [At this] end it had a tail, near four times as long as the whole body.*[4]

Leeuwenhoek called the vorticellae "the most wretched creatures that I have ever seen."[5] He felt sorry for them because they seemed to get their tails caught on things all the time. When this happened, he said,

> *they pulled their body out into an oval. . . . [They] struggle[d], by strongly stretching themselves, to get their tail loose. . . . Their whole body then sprang back towards the . . . [end] of the tail. . . . Their tails then coiled up serpent-wise. . . . This . . . stretching out and pulling together of the tail continued.*[6]

Leeuwenhoek wrote about the vorticella again

*Vorticella, a kind of protist, attaches its tail to water plants. It moves up and down and stirs up the water to catch food.*

late in his life. By then he understood the little creatures much better. He most likely had seen them through better microscopes than those he first used.

For one thing, he realized that tiny, hairlike structures went all around the top of each vorticella's bell-shaped body. These hairs formed a circle. From some angles, the hairs at the ends of the circle looked bunched together. These bunches were what he had thought were horns. (He had not seen the other hairs at all.) He now knew that these hairs stirred up the water, which brought food bits to the animal.

He no longer felt so sorry for the vorticellae. He knew that their tails were not caught by accident. Instead, the animals attached themselves to water plants. They moved up and down to escape danger or catch food.

Leeuwenhoek found some of the most interesting microbes in what he called pepper-water. He had wondered what made pepper taste so hot. He thought bits of pepper might be shaped like tiny needles. They might be so sharp

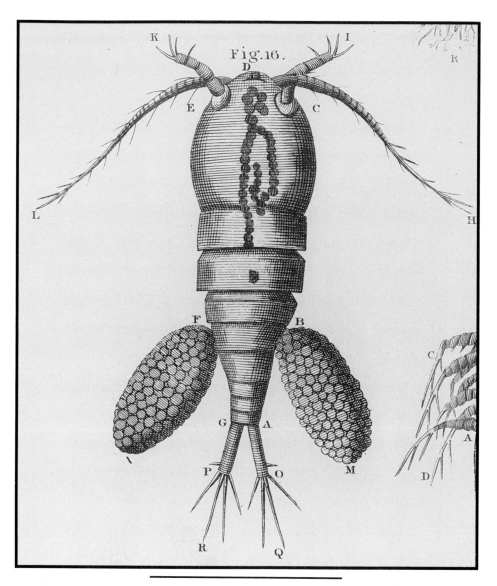

*In addition to microbes, Leeuwenhoek studied larger creatures that lived in water, such as this shrimplike animal. It was tiny but could perhaps be seen with the naked eye.*

that they hurt the tongue. To find out if this was so, he soaked pepper in water for three weeks. He wanted to make it soft. Then the large pieces might come apart, and he could examine them.

On April 24, 1676, Leeuwenhoek looked at the pepper-water under a microscope. To his surprise, he found four kinds of microbes in it. One kind, he wrote, "were incredibly small. . . . I judged that if a hundred of them . . . lay stretched out one by another, they would not equal the length of a coarse grain of sand. . . . Ten hundred thousand of them . . . could not equal the dimensions [volume] of a grain of such coarse sand."[7] The only living things this small are bacteria. Leeuwenhoek was the first to see them.

In later letters, Leeuwenhoek described other kinds of microscopic living things. Some, he said, shot through the water like pike, fast-moving fish. Others looked like snakes. They "moved by bending, as an eel swims." But, he added, "an eel always swims with the head first. . . . These tiny animals swim as well backwards as forwards."[8]

Leeuwenhoek even noted that vinegar killed the little animals in pepper-water. He may have been the first to describe a substance that killed microbes.

The Royal Society had trouble believing Leeuwenhoek's reports about the little animals. To convince the doubters, Leeuwenhoek sent the society letters from eight men. They included ministers, lawyers, and doctors. The men signed the letters under oath. All swore they had seen the little creatures.

The British scientists still wanted to see for themselves. They made their own pepper-water. They looked at it under microscopes, but they found no living things.

If anyone could settle the question, the group thought, it would be Robert Hooke. By then Hooke was a chief officer of the society. He had not used microscopes for years. Still, the group asked him to repeat Leeuwenhoek's experiments.

Hooke did so late in 1677. Using his old microscopes, he looked at water in which pepper or grain had been soaked. He found "very small creatures swimming up and down" in these mixtures.[9]

Hooke showed the creatures to the society at several meetings. On November 15 a member named Birch recorded, "There was no longer any doubt of Mr. Leeuwenhoek's discovery."[10]

This was not true outside the society. Over the years, many people questioned this part of Leeuwenhoek's work. Some were visiting scientists. Others were neighbors in Delft. Leeuwenhoek grew used to hearing that he told "fairy-tales about the little animals."[11] Still, he swore he had seen all he claimed—and more. On November 12, 1680, he wrote,

> *I . . . can as plainly see [the smallest of] them . . . as with the naked eye we behold . . . gnats sporting in the open air. . . . I see some of them [larger animals] open their mouths . . . I have discovered hairs at the mouths of some of these species [kinds].*[12]

How did these microbes get into water? Some people thought they were made from nonliving matter. Leeuwenhoek was sure this was wrong. They had to be born from parents like themselves.

He thought they might be carried on the dust that floats in the air. He found that some microbes could live for a long time in dried form. He thought they might be drawn up into the air when water dried up. Then, when it rained, they might be brought back down from the clouds with the rainwater. Some microbes do move from place to place in this way.

Finding microbes in water was startling enough, but Leeuwenhoek went on to spot them in the bodies of people as well. In a letter dated September 17, 1683, he described the ones he found on people's teeth.

He started with his own teeth. He told the Royal Society that he cleaned his teeth daily. This, he knew, was not common. Because he did so, he wrote, "my teeth are . . . clean and white. . . . Few persons of my age [fifty-one] can show so good a set." Still, he could see in a mirror that a "white substance . . . like a mixture of flour and water" stuck to his teeth.[13] He saw it mostly on the back ones. Dentists now call this substance plaque. It is made of food bits, saliva (spit), and bacteria.

Leeuwenhoek guessed that little animals might live in this matter. He scraped some off and mixed it with his saliva. That made it thin enough to see through. He then saw "many very small animalcules. . . . The largest sort . . . [was] leaping about in the fluid like the fish called a jack. . . . The second sort . . . had a . . . whirling motion." A third kind were too small for him to make out their shape. They moved like "gnats, or flies, sporting in the air."[14]

He went on to look at matter from other people's mouths. One was an old man who said he had "never washed his mouth in all his life."[15] Leeuwenhoek found that people who never cleaned their teeth had the most animals. He guessed that these creatures caused such people's "stinking" breath, but even clean mouths held microbes by the millions. "All the people living in our United Netherlands," he wrote, "are not as many as the living animals that I carry in my own mouth this very day."[16]

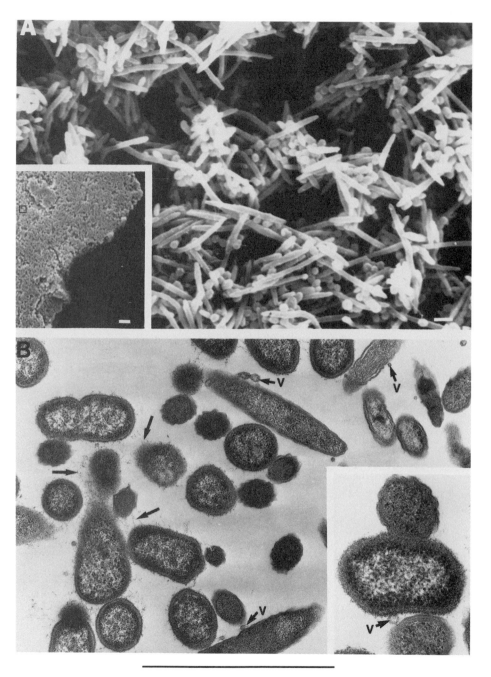

*Even a clean mouth is full of bacteria like these. Leeuwenhoek was the first to see bacteria in tooth plaque.*

There was nothing Leeuwenhoek would not look at. Once he was sick and had loose bowel movements. He studied those, too! On November 12, 1680, he wrote that he had found little animals there as well. "Their bodies were somewhat longer than broad. . . . Their belly, which was flat-like, . . . [had] little paws. . . . They made . . . a stir in the clear medium [fluid]."[17]

These creatures had probably made Leeuwenhoek sick. Most likely they were a kind of protist called *Giardia* that lives in the intestine. People still get sick from drinking *Giardia* in dirty water.

Leeuwenhoek never seemed to guess, though, that his "little animals" might cause illness. This may have been because he found them in so many places. They were in the bodies of healthy people and animals. They were in water that people could drink without getting sick. Most of the ones he saw were in fact harmless.

In 1693, one visitor claimed that Leeuwenhoek had discovered "more kinds of invisible animals than the world before him knew there were visible ones."[18] This was an exaggeration—but perhaps not by much.

Leeuwenhoek himself was delighted by his "little animals." He wrote that "among all the marvels that I have discovered in nature, [these are] the most marvelous of all."[19] Many modern scientists would agree with him.

# Creepy-Crawlies

ANTONI VAN LEEUWENHOEK'S NEIGHBORS
might have been shocked to learn what was in his
pockets. Why, they would have wondered, did he
carry around a box of tiny worms?

Carrying worms in his pocket helped
Leeuwenhoek study the lives of insects. The
"worms" were larvae, the young of certain insects.
He had watched them hatch from eggs. He knew
they must have warmth to stay alive. He found just
one way to keep them warm in cold Dutch winters.
That was to put them next to his body.

Sometimes he even got other family members
to help. Once he asked his wife to keep a box of

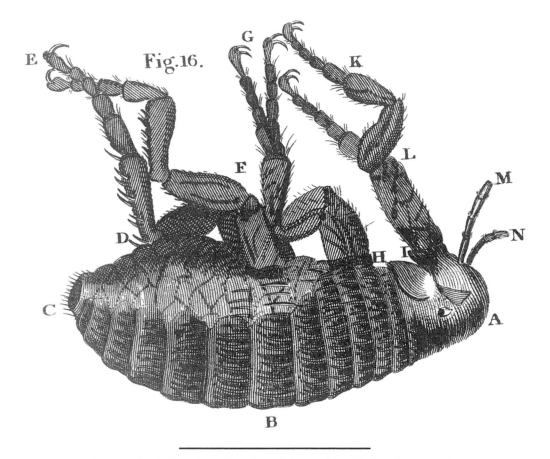

Fig.16.

*Leeuwenhoek let adult fleas like this one bite his hand to get the blood they needed. He killed flies to feed the larvae.*

silkworm eggs under her clothes. (Silkworms are the young of a kind of moth.) Another time she did the same with a box of mites. She must have been a patient woman!

Leeuwenhoek studied sixty-seven kinds of insects. He also looked at other small living things, such as spiders and shrimp. He tried to learn all about them. He watched them grow from eggs to adults. At each stage of their lives, he put them under his microscopes.

He had no trouble finding insects to look at. Ants lived in his backyard. Insect pests showed up in apples from his orchard. When he wanted to study fleas, he just asked the maid to catch some around the house. Tiny mites infested stored food in his kitchen. Lice he had to buy, but "I had plenty of them brought to me for my money."[1]

Carrying larvae or eggs in his pocket wasn't all Leeuwenhoek went through to study insects. He killed flies to feed his flea larvae. He put up with stings so he could see inside an ants' nest. (He wrote that the stings "gave me more pain than in

my life before I had experienced from them.")[2]
He knew that adult fleas and lice had to drink
fresh blood, so he let them bite his hands.

Only once were Leeuwenhoek's experiments
too much for him. He wanted to learn how many
young lice would appear in a certain length of
time. He therefore put two female lice into a clean
sock and wore it. He used a black sock instead of
his usual white one. He hoped the lice and their
eggs would show up clearly on the dark cloth. He
used strips of another sock to tie the first one shut
at the knee so the lice could not escape.

After six days, he found that each female had
laid about fifty eggs in the sock. He then put the
sock back on, eggs and all, for another ten days.
By that time, he found that about twenty-five of
the eggs had hatched into young lice. More were
ready to hatch.

Leeuwenhoek did not wait for them. He knew
he was just "enduring, in one leg, what most poor
people . . . suffer in their whole bodies . . . all their
lives." Still, he had had enough. As he told the
Royal Society, "I was . . . disgusted at the sight of

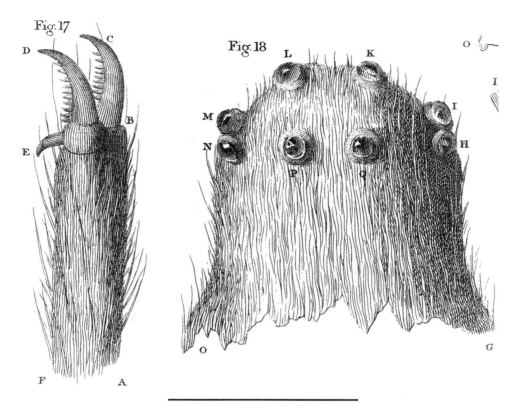

*Seen under Leeuwenhoek's microscope, a spider looks like a monster from outer space. His artist's drawings show the spider's leg, with a claw, and its head, with several eyes.*

so many lice. . . . I threw the stocking containing them into the street."[3] After that, he "rubbed [his] leg and foot very hard" to kill any lice still there. Then he went back to clean white stockings.

When Leeuwenhoek studied an insect or other creature, he did more than watch it grow up. He carried out experiments to learn how its body worked. He did this with spiders, for instance. (Spiders are arachnids, not insects. They are related to insects, though.)

Most spiders spin webs from silky threads. Leeuwenhoek wanted to know how they made these threads. He saw that the thread came from the rear of a spider's body, but was there one thread, or several? At first he could not tell.

Leeuwenhoek found a way to glue a spider on its back. Now it could not move the rear part of its body. Then he used a tiny tool like tweezers "to draw out from the body, that small part of the thread which projected from the organ . . . from which the threads proceed."[4] This organ is now called a spinneret. He later found that each spider had eight groups of spinnerets. He thought there were over four hundred spinnerets in all.

Leeuwenhoek learned that each set of spinnerets put out "a great number of exceeding[ly] small threads."[5] A short distance from the spider's body, these threads twist together. They form one or two thicker threads. The strands of a rope are twisted in the same way. The twisting makes the rope strong. Spider silk is also very strong. Leeuwenhoek guessed that the twisting made it so.

Leeuwenhoek also studied the way spiders attacked enemies and prey. He found that they do not sting, as some people thought. Instead, they bite with the pointed fangs in their heads. He saw a small hole in the end of each fang. He guessed that poison could flow out through this hole, and he was right.

Sometimes Leeuwenhoek put two or three spiders in the same tube. He saw that small ones tried to get away from large ones. Two of the same size, though, would fight. "Neither would give way. . . . Both of them grappled together furiously with their fangs, till one . . . lay dead," he wrote.[6] He noted that female spiders attacked males, even at mating time.

Leeuwenhoek liked to find out whether common beliefs about animals were true. People knew, for instance, that ants took food into their nests. Most people thought the ants stored the food so they would have enough to eat in the winter. Even the Bible praised ants for working hard and planning ahead. Leeuwenhoek wondered whether this was what the ants were really doing.

To find out, Leeuwenhoek opened up an ant nest in his garden. (That was when he got stung.) He watched the ants store food in the nest. He became sure the food was "for the maggots [ant larvae], . . . who cannot . . . feed themselves."[7] He doubted that the ants needed food in the winter. He knew that some other insects could survive all winter without eating. They went into hibernation, a kind of sleep. He thought ants probably did this, too.

Once some Englishmen visited Leeuwenhoek. They mentioned that English people said that someone who did not understand something was "blind as a beetle."[8] This saying must have made Leeuwenhoek laugh. He showed the men that a beetle is not blind at all.

A beetle has two large eyes. Each is shaped like half of a ball. Leeuwenhoek showed the men a beetle's eye through a microscope. Now they could see that the eye was made up of many smaller eyes. Today, the two large eyes are called compound eyes. The smaller eyes are simple eyes. Leeuwenhoek calculated that a beetle had 3,181 eyes in all.

Many insects have compound eyes. Once Leeuwenhoek looked at a moth's compound eye through a microscope. He wrote, "All the surrounding objects were clearly to be seen through each of the small optical organs [simple eyes]. . . . The great . . . steeple of our new church in Delft, which is 300 feet high, . . . appeared no larger than the point of a small needle."[9]

Leeuwenhoek was not afraid to change his mind when his eyes told him his ideas were wrong. He had to do this when he looked at the strange swellings, called galls, that grew on some kinds of trees.

Leeuwenhoek first saw galls on an oak tree. He thought they were the tree's fruit, but he noticed that they grew on the leaves. That was an odd place for fruit to appear. Also, some leaves had several galls, while others had none. Fruit is not arranged this way.

He finally decided that the galls had been

made by insects. To check his idea, he cut open some galls. Sure enough, each had a tiny hole in the middle. Inside the hole was "a living white worm, which had very little motion."[10] This worm was an insect larva.

Leeuwenhoek studied galls at different times of year. In time, he worked out the whole life cycle of the insect that made them. It was a tiny fly. The adult fly laid its eggs on an oak leaf. When the larvae hatched, Leeuwenhoek thought, they bit into the large vessels of the leaf. Water and nutrients oozed out of the leaf. They formed a swelling around each larva. (Almost always he found just one larva in each gall.) The gall made food for the larva. The larva finally changed into an adult. The adult fly dug its way out of the gall and flew away. In galls that contained no larvae, he often saw the small hole that the escaping fly had left.

Some of Leeuwenhoek's insect studies had practical uses. For instance, he looked at a kind of moth whose larvae ate grain. This moth was a pest. In a letter dated March 7, 1692, he described a way to control it.

Burning sulfur would kill this kind of moth, Leeuwenhoek wrote. He figured out how much would be needed to kill the moths in a granary (grain storehouse) of a certain size. He then tested his plan in a real granary filled with moths. He set the sulfur on fire. Then he left, shutting the door. He knew the sulfur smoke could poison people as well as moths.

Leeuwenhoek checked the granary two days later. He found that most of the moths were dead, but a few were still alive. That did not mean his treatment was a failure, he said. Part of the problem was that some windows in the granary had been broken. That let a lot of the smoke escape.

Also, some moths had been in their pupa stage while the granary was filled with smoke. This is the stage in which many insects' bodies change from larva to adult form. A hard case most often protects the insect while these changes happen. The cases had saved the moths from the poison.

Because of what he had learned, Leeuwenhoek changed his directions for the sulfur treatment.

He said it should be started as soon as the first moths were seen. This way, the moths would have no time to lay eggs. It should also be repeated several times. Then all the moths would be killed.

Leeuwenhoek was glad when helpful ideas

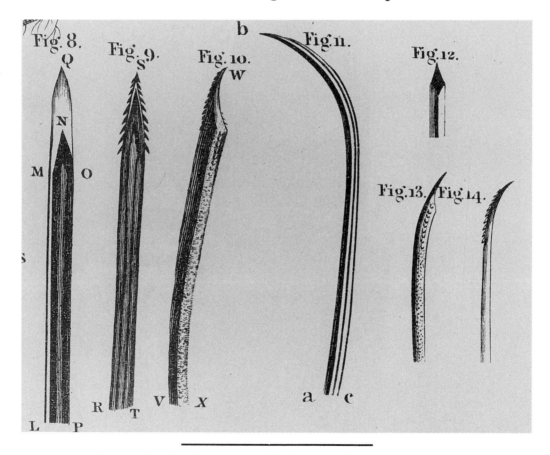

*Leeuwenhoek often compared the same feature in different animals. These drawings show the stingers of several kinds of gnats and horseflies.*

came from his studies. They were not the main reason he used his microscopes to look at insects, though. He just wanted to discover the tiny details of nature. Over and over he exclaimed at the beauty of what he saw. He praised the hairs on a fly and the "feathers" (scales) on a gnat's wing. Speaking of a fly, he wrote, "there is greater cause for admiration . . . in . . . so small . . . an animal, than in . . . a horse or an ox."[11]

# 5

# Inside the Body

(optional)

ANTONI VAN LEEUWENHOEK PICKED UP A
fiercely flapping rooster. He wrapped it in a cloth
to stop its struggles. Only its head stuck out. He
looked as if he were planning a chicken dinner,
but in fact he was trying to solve a mystery that
had puzzled many scientists for fifty years.

In 1628 an English scientist named William
Harvey had published a book that told how the
blood moved through the body. Harvey showed
that the heart pumped the blood. It pushed blood
out through vessels, or tubes, called arteries. The
blood flowed through and nourished the body.
Then it went back to the heart in other vessels

called veins. In short, the blood moved in circuits. No one before Harvey had known this.

One puzzle remained, though. Harvey could not see how the blood got from arteries to veins. Marcello Malpighi (mal-PEE-gee), an Italian scientist, had solved this mystery in 1660. That was three years after Harvey's death. Using a microscope, Malpighi saw tiny blood vessels, now called capillaries, in frogs' lungs. They joined arteries to veins. They completed the circle that Harvey had described. Harvey could not see them because he had no microscope.

Harvey's work was well known. Malpighi's was less so, and Leeuwenhoek had not heard of it. As far as he knew, the puzzle of blood circulation still had a piece missing. He hoped to find that piece.

Red flaps of skin called wattles hung from the rooster's neck. Leeuwenhoek knew that blood vessels filled the wattles. Blood showed clearly through the wattles' thin skin, making them red. He put a microscope against the wattles. He hoped he would see the tiny connecting vessels inside.

It didn't work. He had no better luck when he studied a rabbit's ear. Leeuwenhoek finally decided that no one could see these blood vessels in land animals. Even at the thinnest parts, their bodies and skins were too thick.

He got better results with tadpoles, the fishlike young of frogs. In a tadpole's tail, he saw that "the blood . . . was conveyed through . . . minute [tiny] vessels from the middle of the tail toward the edge. . . . Each of these vessels had a curve. . . . [It] carried the blood back towards the middle of the tail." The curved part of each vessel joined an artery to a vein. "And thus it appears," Leeuwenhoek wrote, "that an artery and a vein are . . . the same vessel."[1]

Leeuwenhoek also saw capillaries in the tails of small, snakelike fish called eels. An eel's tail fin, he wrote, "looked as if . . . it was composed of nothing but blood vessels."[2] He decided that eels' tails were the best places for people to see blood circulation. He even made a special device for showing this. It was a microscope attached to a tube that held a small eel.

Leeuwenhoek studied blood itself as well as blood movement. He first described blood in a letter sent to the Royal Society on April 7, 1674.

The first blood Leeuwenhoek studied was his own. He pricked his hand with a needle. He put the opening of a glass tube against the drop of blood that came out. Some of the blood ran up into the tube. He could then mount the tube on a microscope and look at the blood. Sometimes he spread the blood on a glass plate instead.

Part of the blood, Leeuwenhoek wrote, was a watery fluid. It is now called serum. Floating in this fluid were round particles. He called them globules.

Seen one by one, the blood globules had little color. Several together, though, looked reddish. Leeuwenhoek guessed, rightly, that they were what made blood look red. These globules are known today as red blood cells. They carry oxygen through the body.

As always, Leeuwenhoek tried to measure these tiny objects. He said that one red cell was twenty-five-thousand times smaller in volume

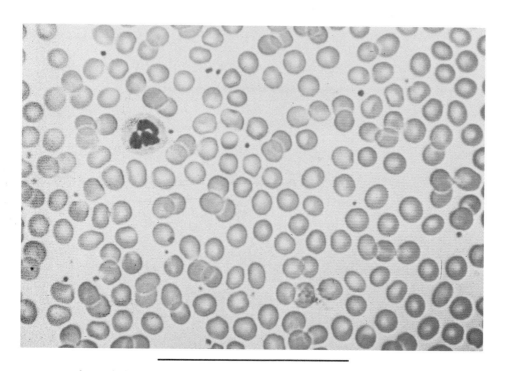

*These disk-shaped cells make blood look red. Leeuwenhoek was the first to see red blood cells, though his view of them probably wasn't as clear as this modern photo.*

than a fine grain of sand. That would make it about 1/3200 of an inch across. Modern measurements show that he was almost exactly right.

Leeuwenhoek compared blood cells in many kinds of animals. He found that even when the animals were very different in size, their blood cells were not. He wrote that red cells were "no larger in a whale than in the smallest fish."[3]

The red cells did differ in shape, though. The

ones in human blood were round, Leeuwenhoek said. (They are really flat disks.) By contrast, those in fish and frogs were oval.

Leeuwenhoek also found another difference in fish cells. He wrote on March 3, 1682, that he saw "a little round body" in some of them.[4] Human red cells did not have these bodies.

The structure Leeuwenhoek saw was the cell's nucleus. Most cells have a nucleus. (Human red cells are among the few that don't.) The nucleus acts like the brain of a cell. It controls what the cell does. Leeuwenhoek did not understand what a cell nucleus was. Still, he was the first person to see and describe it.

Leeuwenhoek also studied animals' eyes. The part he looked at most was the hard, clear part near the front of the eye that looks like a piece of glass or crystal. He called it the crystalline body. It is now called the lens. Like the lenses in microscopes, the eye lens focuses light. (It does not make things look larger, though.)

Leeuwenhoek looked mostly at lenses from the eyes of cows. He saw that the lenses were almost, but not quite, round. On April 14, 1684, he wrote that a lens was like "a small globe . . . made up of thin pieces of paper, laid one on another."[5] Each paperlike layer was made of thin strands or fibers that lay side by side in "a very neat arrangement."[6] Each layer was one fiber thick. He guessed that each lens had about two thousand layers.

Leeuwenhoek noted that when the lens is taken from the eye right after death, "no glass exceeds it in transparency." It is so clear, he said, because the layers and fibers are arranged in such an orderly way. This arrangement lets light "go straight through it [the lens]. . . . If this were not the case, the crystalline body would not . . . be transparent but white."[7]

Leeuwenhoek also studied body tissues. A tissue is made of cells that look alike and do the same job. Muscle is one kind of tissue, nerves are another, and bone is a third. Leeuwenhoek looked at all of these.

Muscles make the body move by contracting (squeezing together) and relaxing. If you bend your arm, you can feel the muscles in your upper arm bulge as they contract. Muscles can contract because they are made of fibers that can slide past each other. Under a microscope, some parts of the fibers are dark in color, and some are light. This makes muscle tissue look striped.

Leeuwenhoek looked at muscles in a cow. (Steak is mostly cow muscle.) He noticed their striped look. He described the stripes as "rings and wrinkles."[8]

He also saw the fibers in muscle. He wrote that the fibers lay side by side, as if woven together. Each fiber, he said, was twenty-five times thinner than a hair. Fifty of them, put side by side, would cover just 1/22 of an inch.

Muscle fibers, Leeuwenhoek noted, were grouped in bundles. Each bundle was wrapped in a thin membrane (covering). These membranes were attached to a thicker membrane. It wrapped the whole muscle.

Leeuwenhoek looked at muscles in animals ranging from whales to fleas. He was the first to describe the muscle fibers of so many animals in such detail. He was also the first to measure them.

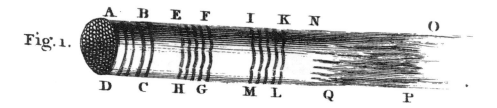

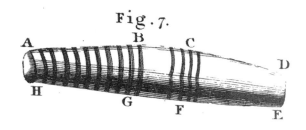

*Leeuwenhoek noticed that muscle fibers look striped. He said they were marked with "rings and wrinkles."*

He found that the muscle fibers in a whale were no bigger than those in a small fish.

Leeuwenhoek also studied the special muscle tissue in the heart. He looked at the hearts of ducks, sheep, and several other animals. He described these in April 1694. In the heart, he said, membranes did not divide the muscle fibers into bundles. Instead, "all the fleshy particles [muscle fibers] . . . are . . . chained or linked together."[9]

One part of, say, an arm could be hurt without harming the rest, Leeuwenhoek said. This was not true of the heart, because all its fibers were connected. "When any one particle in the fleshy substance of the heart . . . is wounded, the whole . . . heart . . . suffers."[10] This is why even a small wound to the heart can cause death.

Nerves were another tissue Leeuwenhoek studied. He wrote about the nerves of cows and sheep in his last letter to the Royal Society.

Other scientists had claimed that nerves were hollow. They thought nerves were large tubes, like blood vessels. Leeuwenhoek said the hole in the middle of a nerve was not real. It appeared because nerve tissue shrank as it dried. A nerve was really made of many small tubes. He thought the tubes carried some kind of liquid. His description is correct, except that nerves do not hold liquid. They carry electric signals between body and brain.

Bones and teeth also looked as if they were made of small tubes lying next to each other, Leeuwenhoek said. They look like this under a

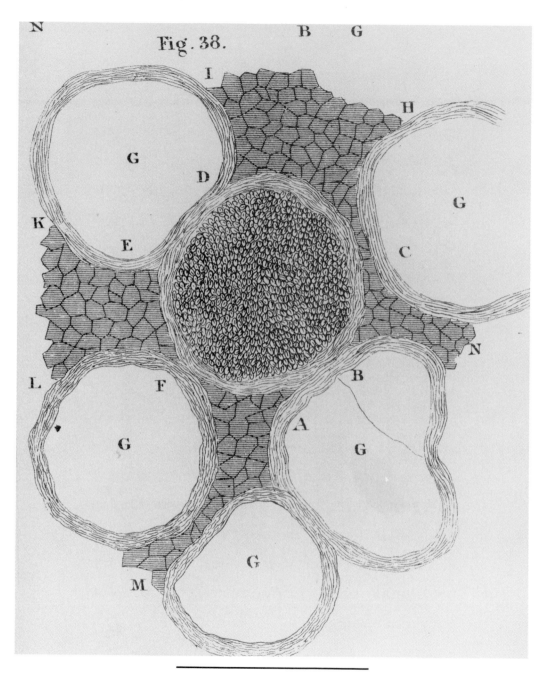

Fig. 38.

*Nerve tissue is made of groups of small tubes that look hollow after the tissue has dried.*

modern microscope, too. The tubes in bone, he noted, ran lengthwise. Those in teeth ran crosswise. They started from the center of the tooth and went outward. He noticed a hollow channel in the center of each tooth. This is where the blood vessels and nerves run.

Leeuwenhoek looked at skin and hair as well. On September 17, 1683, he wrote that the outer part of the skin was covered with scales that looked something like the scales on a fish. He saw that the scales were thicker on some parts of the body than on others. The dead cells on the outer part of the skin do have a scaly look under a microscope. They are not formed in the same way as fish scales, though.

Leeuwenhoek looked at his own hair. He also studied the hair of pigs, sheep, and other animals. He wrote that "hairs are formed with a kind of coat," like the bark on a tree.[11] He saw that a hair has an outer and an inner part. He also saw that a hair is thicker and softer near the root than it is at the tip.

Scientists of Leeuwenhoek's time could not

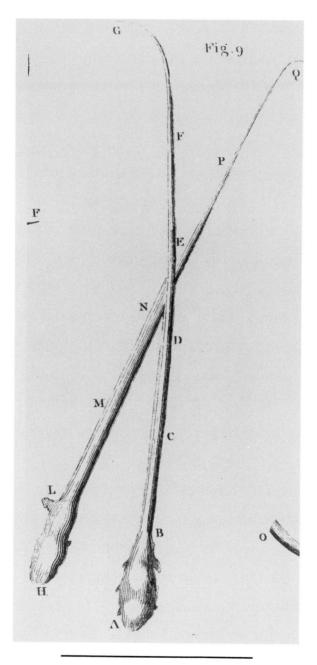

*These human hairs may have come from Leeuwenhoek's beard or his arm. He noticed that hairs grew from the rounded root, not the pointed tip.*

agree about how hairs grew. Some thought they grew mostly at the top, like a sprouting plant. Others said most of the growth took place near the root or bottom of the hair. This root is buried in the skin. Studying the hair on his own face, Leeuwenhoek decided that hairs grow from the root. He was right.

Some doctors today study body tissues under a microscope. Changes in tissues can show why a person is sick. A study of healthy tissues shows how the body works. In looking at tissues, these doctors are following in the footsteps of Antoni van Leeuwenhoek.

# The Beginnings of Life

KILL A BULL AND BURY IT WITH JUST ITS horns showing. Come back a month later and saw off one of the horns. A swarm of bees will fly out.

Stick a dirty shirt in a bin of wheat. Leave it there three weeks. Mice will grow from the shirt and the wheat.

Most people of Leeuwenhoek's time believed that things like this could happen. They thought "lower" forms of life, such as worms and insects, did not need parents. They could be made from mud or decaying matter. This belief went back to ancient times.

Leeuwenhoek strongly disagreed with this

idea. He was sure all living things came from parents like themselves. "A flea or a louse," he wrote, "can no more come . . . from . . . dirt than a horse from a dunghill [waste heap]."[1] He was determined to prove that no living thing could be made from nonliving matter. To do so, he worked out each creature's life cycle.

One insect Leeuwenhoek studied in this way was the corn weevil. This insect got into places where wheat or corn was stored. It was a pest because it ate the grain. People thought the weevils must be made from the grain. After all, they said, weevils appeared in new granaries. Where did they come from, if not the grain?

The answer to that question, Leeuwenhoek wrote on August 6, 1687, was easy. People brought grain from old granaries to new ones. Weevils were tiny. The people could easily carry them in on their clothes without knowing it. The cart that brought the grain might also hold weevils. So might the grain itself.

To prove that weevils came from weevil parents, Leeuwenhoek had set out to trace their life cycle. Near the end of March, he wrote, he saw some weevils mating. He put them in a container with airholes. He gave them wheat grains for food. In mid-June he saw "two short and thick little maggots" in one container.[2] These were the weevils' larvae. He cut apart some of the adult weevils. He found eggs in the bodies of the females. The larvae must have hatched from eggs like these.

He looked at the wheat grains under a microscope. One seemed to be whole. Still, the microscope showed small holes in it. Inside this grain he found an adult weevil.

In time, Leeuwenhoek watched the weevils' whole life. He found single eggs laid inside grains of wheat. Part of the grain around each egg was broken down to powder. This made food for the larva. After the larvae hatched, he saw them slowly grow into adult weevils. "The beak, horns, and claws appear[ed] by degrees."[3] He wrote, "I trust that these . . . observations will prove that weevils cannot be produced otherwise than by . . . [mating] and laying eggs."[4]

Part of Leeuwenhoek's objection to the belief that living things could be made from nonliving matter was scientific. Each time he looked for eggs and parents, he found them. Another part was religious. God, he believed, had made all the types of living things long ago. All things living now had to be descended from the ones created then.

Leeuwenhoek also had seen that all living things were complex. To him, they were beautiful. He just could not believe that such beauty could come from rotting matter. In 1692, for instance, he described a moth. He wrote that it was "provided by nature with the means to propagate its species [reproduce its kind], furnished with eyes exquisitely formed, with horns, with tufts of feathers on its head, with wings covered with . . . multitudes of feathers [scales]."

Then he asked, "Can this moth, . . . adorned with so many beauties, be produced from corruption [decay]?"[5] To him, the only possible answer was no.

Not all living things created young in the same

way, Leeuwenhoek found. He discovered some ways that no one had seen before. He reported that some one-celled creatures reproduced by splitting in half, for instance.

Leeuwenhoek also learned that a small water creature called a hydra made young by budding. Sometimes he saw small hydras attached to larger ones. At first he thought this was an accident. Then he noticed that the small hydras slowly grew larger, finally letting go of the larger hydra and swimming away. He rightly guessed that he was seeing a form of reproduction.

Most living things, though, had two parents. One was a male, the other a female. Scientists of the time disagreed strongly about what each parent gave to the offspring.

People knew that females' bodies made eggs. They were less sure what the males did. William Harvey had written that he could not find anything that a male left in a female's body after mating. The male, he thought, must give some spirit or life force that could not be seen. It made the egg start growing into a new living thing.

Harvey did not have a microscope, but Leeuwenhoek did. He used it to look at semen, the thick fluid that comes from a male's sex organ during mating. In November 1677 he told the Royal Society that semen was full of "little

British scientist William Harvey thought only the egg was important in making a new living thing. Leeuwenhoek thought the same of the sperm. Each had half of the truth.

animals," something like the ones he had seen in water.

These "animals" looked like tiny tadpoles. "Their bodies were round. [They] were blunt in front and ran to a point behind," Leeuwenhoek wrote. Each had "a thin tail, about five or six times as long as the body. . . . They moved forward owing to the motion of their tails. [It was] like that of a snake or an eel swimming in water."[6] The semen "animals" were smaller than red blood cells. He thought a million of them would not have the volume of a large grain of sand.

Leeuwenhoek had discovered sperm cells, the male sex cells. These cells bring information from the male to the female. This information will help the young animal develop. So will information in the egg cell, which comes from the female.

Semen is packed with sperm cells, Leeuwenhoek found. He thought there were "more than ten animals in the milt [semen] of a cod [a kind of fish] . . . [for each] human being on the earth's surface."[7] He knew, though, that very few of these would form offspring. In the same way, just a few of a plant's many seeds become new plants.

Leeuwenhoek knew the sperm cells were important. He studied them again and again. He wrote about them in 57 of his 280 published letters. He looked at sperm cells from thirty kinds of animals. He found that, like red blood cells, sperm cells were about the same size in all animals.

Leeuwenhoek's find thrilled him so much that it led him to make a mistake. Harvey could not see sperm, so he had thought that only eggs were important. Leeuwenhoek came to hold the opposite view. He thought all life came from sperm. The female's only job, he said, was to give food and shelter to the sperm as it grew into a new living thing. One reason he made this mistake was that egg cells did not move on their own. Sperm cells did. Things that did not move did not seem alive to Leeuwenhoek.

Leeuwenhoek thought all parts of the future offspring were contained in the sperm. Some other scientists soon took this belief a step further. They claimed they could see tiny, manlike figures in human sperm. Leeuwenhoek himself never made this claim. He pointed out that a seed does not look like a tree, though it will become a tree. In the same way, he said, it was "wrong to assert that the little worms [sperm cells] in the human sperm [semen] are small babies, even though a child is formed from such a small worm."[8]

Some scientists agreed with Leeuwenhoek about the importance of sperm. Others did not. Leeuwenhoek and his old friend Reinier de Graaf often argued about this. De Graaf, like Harvey, thought the egg was most important in forming offspring. De Graaf agreed that sperm cells were alive. He didn't think they contained a future

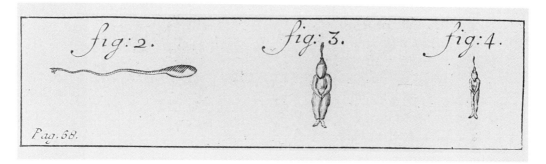

*A sperm cell has the tadpole shape seen on the left. Some scientists of Leeuwenhoek's time thought they could see human figures in the sperm, like the drawings in the middle and right. Leeuwenhoek said this was nonsense.*

living thing, though. He said their job was to bring the matter in the egg to life.

Over a hundred years later, scientists realized that Leeuwenhoek and de Graaf each had half of the truth. Both a sperm cell and an egg cell are needed to form a new life. After mating, one of the male's sperm cells enters an egg cell in the female's body. The result is a combined cell called the fertilized egg. This cell will grow and divide to become the offspring. The body parts of the young animal do not physically appear in either the sperm or the egg. They exist only in the form of information.

# The Great Man of the Century

THE MORE THE ROYAL SOCIETY SAW OF Leeuwenhoek's work, the more impressed the group became. Finally, on February 8, 1680, the society made him a Fellow, a full member. This meant they thought him as good a scientist as any in Europe.

Leeuwenhoek knew this for the honor it was. He wrote a letter of thanks to the society. In it he promised "to strive with all my might and main, all my life long, to make myself worthy of this . . . privilege."[1]

Becoming a member of the Royal Society sealed Leeuwenhoek's fame. Later in 1680, a friend named Constantijn Huygens (KON-stan-teen HI-genz) wrote, "Everybody here is still rushing to visit Leeuwenhoek. [They see him] as the great man of the century."[2]

During the rest of Leeuwenhoek's life, people came from all over Europe to meet him in Delft. Some were scientists, others were nobles or even royalty. All wanted to see the wonders revealed by his microscope. For the most part, he made them welcome.

Of the kings and queens who visited Leeuwenhoek, the best known may have been Peter the Great. A tall, handsome man, Peter was the tsar (emperor) of Russia. He wanted to bring European ways to his country, and he was most interested in science.

Peter came to Europe in 1698. One country he visited was Holland. Traveling on the Dutch canals, he stopped at Delft. He asked Leeuwenhoek to come to his boat. Leeuwenhoek seldom left home, but he did so for Peter.

Leeuwenhoek's visit lasted two hours. He showed Peter and his nobles the blood movement in an eel's tail. Peter said he was "delighted" with this and other sights.[3] Leeuwenhoek even may have given the tsar a microscope or two. (One later turned up in Russia.) This was an honor worthy of an emperor. The Dutchman almost never gave his microscopes away.

In his later years, Leeuwenhoek became more popular than he liked to be. In 1711, he complained that twenty-six people had come to see him in four days. So many visitors, he said, "made me so tired that I broke out in a sweat."[4]

By this time, Leeuwenhoek lived with only his grown daughter, Maria. Cornelia, his second wife, had died in 1693. Maria never married. She spent her life taking care of her eccentric father and running their home.

Leeuwenhoek began to limit the number of people he would see. "If I should receive everyone who comes to my house, I should have no freedom at all," he wrote.[5] He asked one German visitor to tell no one that he had been let in. "He is old, and tired of being pestered," the German noted.[6]

*Even kings and queens came to see Leeuwenhoek's wonderful microscopes. In this painting he is showing some to Queen Catherine of England, the wife of Charles II.*

(Leeuwenhoek was sixty-seven years old at the time.)

Leeuwenhoek's growing dislike of visitors came from more than tiredness. Certain past guests, he felt, had mistreated him. Some had claimed his ideas as their own. Others had made fun of him because of his lack of education. He said criticism did not bother him. It seems to have made him more reluctant to meet strangers, though.

In fact, in spite of his many callers, Leeuwenhoek was rather cut off from other scientists. He worked alone. He could not read the languages in which most scientific papers were written. He thus knew little about what others were doing.

This separation was both a strength and a weakness. On the good side, it meant that Leeuwenhoek was not swayed by what others believed. Sometimes, though, it led him to make mistakes. "Being ignorant of all other men's thoughts, he is wholly trusting to his own," Thomas Molyneux wrote. "Now and then [this] leads him into . . . suggest[ing] very odd accounts of things."[7]

Leeuwenhoek's lack of education sometimes formed a wall of distrust between him and other scientists. This was worst with those who came from universities. When Leeuwenhoek first wrote to the Royal Society, he had apologized for his lack of training. Later, though, he became almost proud of it. "Men are apt to hold fast by what their teachers have impressed on 'em," he wrote.[8] He felt that he was free of such prejudice.

He also distrusted students' reasons for entering science. He thought most did so just to gain fame or money. He said they would never work as hard as he had. Worst of all, he felt, they were not "curious to know."[9] Without this love of learning, he felt, they could not be true scientists.

Some trained scientists, in turn, distrusted Leeuwenhoek. They said he did not really understand what he saw. In this they were partly right. Scientists are taught to see relationships among facts and ideas. They learn to place things in a framework or system. For the most part, Leeuwenhoek did not do this. He never learned to organize his work. He could not see the things he found out as part of a larger whole.

Many scientists respected Leeuwenhoek, though. In 1716, the University of Louvain (in what is now Belgium) sent him a silver medal. His portrait was on one side. The other showed a beehive. Around the hive, bees gathered nectar from flowers. Delft appeared in the background.

Bees were famous for their hard work. In effect, the medal compared Leeuwenhoek to a bee. He gathered facts from nature, it seemed to say, as bees took nectar from flowers. He produced knowledge the way bees made honey. With the medal was a poem that praised Leeuwenhoek and his work.

Leeuwenhoek wrote to thank the university. When he thought of their kind words, he said, "I don't only blush, but my eyes filled with tears too." He noted that "my work . . . was not pursued . . . to gain the praise I now enjoy." He said he did it only "from a craving after knowledge."[10]

Leeuwenhoek stayed healthy for most of his long life. His eyes remained sharp. In his later years, though, it hurt him to walk. He also sometimes had stomach problems and trouble breathing. He may have had a lung condition called asthma.

In 1717, Leeuwenhoek sent the Royal Society what he thought would be his last letter. He was eighty-five by then. "My hands grow weak, and suffer from a little shakiness," he wrote.[11] In fact he lived almost six years longer, and he wrote eighteen more letters to the Royal Society.

Leeuwenhoek continued his studies to the very end of his life. Just a day before he died, he dictated a letter to a director of the Dutch East India Company. The director had sent him some sand to look at. He wanted to know whether there was gold in it. Leeuwenhoek reported what he had found. Later still, just a few hours before his death, Leeuwenhoek asked a friend to translate two more letters for the Royal Society.

Antoni van Leeuwenhoek died on August 26, 1723. By then he was almost ninety-one years old. He died of a lung disease, probably pneumonia. A friend saw him in his last days. He reported that "he continued his course cheerfully to the end of his life along the track of Science."[12]

Leeuwenhoek had seldom given his microscopes away while he was alive, but his will ordered a set of twenty-six to be sent to the Royal Society. He had planned this gift for a long time. His daughter, Maria, mailed the microscopes along with a sad little note. She signed it "my father's grief-stricken daughter."[13]

On August 31, 1723, Leeuwenhoek was buried in the Old Church in Delft. He had a fine funeral, with coaches, and sixteen men to carry his coffin. Very likely most of the people of Delft came to say good-bye to their odd but famous neighbor.

Maria had the graves of Leeuwenhoek and his second wife moved to a different part of the church in 1739. She set up a monument over them. The monument can still be seen. It is a memorial to one of the great minds of science, a man who was always "curious to know."

# Afterword:
# A Microscope Pioneer

A FRIEND ONCE TOLD ANTONI VAN Leeuwenhoek, "You've got the truth, but it won't be received [accepted] in your lifetime."[1] In many ways, the friend was right.

Most of Leeuwenhoek's neighbors in Delft never quite believed that what he saw was real. (Late in his life, he complained that they called him a magician. They said he showed people "what don't exist."[2]) They still thought insects could be made from dirt or dung. They doubted that tiny animals lived in water or semen. Many Europeans held these views until the late nineteenth century.

Most scientists did accept Leeuwenhoek's work. Few, though, really understood it. They did not see why it was important. Most did not dream, for instance, that microscopic living things could make people ill.

Even in Leeuwenhoek's lifetime, scientists lost interest in microscopes. Robert Hooke wrote in 1692 that the Dutchman was almost the only person still working with this tool. Few tried to repeat or add to Leeuwenhoek's work for over a hundred years. This was mostly because no one else could make microscopes as good as his.

Leeuwenhoek himself was partly to blame for that. He wouldn't show anyone how he made his microscopes. He wouldn't even let people look at his best ones. When asked why he didn't teach others, he just grumbled, "I can't see there'd be much use."[3]

In the 1840s, compound microscopes finally became as good as the simple ones Leeuwenhoek had made. Then scientists again looked into the world of the very small. Some built on

Leeuwenhoek's work. Others rediscovered things he had found.

Nineteenth-century scientists began to find how cells and tissues worked in the body. They learned that both a sperm and an egg were needed to make a child. They discovered that some microbes could cause sickness. Others, they found, did useful jobs such as breaking down dead matter.

All these discoveries, and many more, grew indirectly from Leeuwenhoek's work. He was the first to describe many of the things that later scientists studied. His detailed, accurate accounts gave them solid ground on which to build.

Leeuwenhoek's discoveries were not his only gift to science. Just as important was the kind of person he was. In many ways he was an ideal scientist.

First, he was a careful observer and recorder. He wrote down each detail, no matter how small. The drawings he ordered were just as detailed. He measured each thing he described.

He worked hard and patiently. He looked at

the same things again and again. He checked them under different conditions. He prepared them in different ways. He compared the same features in dozens of kinds of animals.

He believed only what he saw. He carefully separated what he had seen from what he thought might be true. If he saw things that disagreed with ideas he had formed, he changed his ideas.

He listened to criticism but was not swayed by it. "'Tis not my intention to stick stubbornly to my opinions," he wrote. "As soon as people urge against them any reasonable objections, . . . I'll give [them] up."[4] He would not change his mind just because people disagreed with him, though.

He was "curious to know" about everything. Microbes, body tissues, and insects were just a few of the things he studied. He also looked at plants, minerals, and much more.

He did his work only because he wanted to learn about nature. "No money could ever have driven me to make [my] discoveries," he wrote. "I'm only working out . . . an impulse that was born in me."[5]

Above all, he loved what he did. "In [my] observations . . . I have spent a lot more time than many people would believe," he wrote. "Yet I made them with pleasure."[6] The beauties of nature made him as thrilled as a child. After describing a shrimp, he wrote, "What hidden wonders [there are] in so contemptible [lowly] an animal!"[7] The best scientists today share not only Leeuwenhoek's care in his work but also his joy.

# Activities

LIKE ANTONI VAN LEEUWENHOEK, YOU can do experiments to learn about the world of the very small. You will learn most if you can use a microscope. If you can't get a microscope, use a magnifying glass.

Do these activities. Then try to answer the questions that follow the activities.

## Little Animals

*Materials needed:*

- jars
- water from different places
- dry grass
- black pepper
- glass slide or other flat, clear surface
- eyedropper
- magnifying glass or microscope
- paper and pencil

*Procedure:*

Put clean tap water or rain water in one open jar. In another, put water that has been standing outside for a while. This might come from a pond or stream. It might come from a ditch or puddle in the street. In a third, soak some dry grass in tap water. In a fourth, do the same with black pepper.

Using an eyedropper, take a drop of water from each jar. Put each drop on a glass slide or other flat clear surface. Look at the drop through a microscope or the best magnifying glass you can find. Describe or draw what you see.

Leave the jars outside for a week. Then look at a drop of water from each jar again. Do the same after two weeks, and then after three weeks.

*Questions:*

Do you see anything moving in any of the water drops when you first test them? If so, what does it look like, and how does it move? What changes do you see after one, two, and three weeks? Which jar has the most living things at the end of this time?

## Insect Life Cycle

*Materials needed:*

- insect larvae or eggs
- jar with airholes
- leaves or other food
- magnifying glass or microscope
- paper and pencil or crayons

*Procedure:*

Look in your yard or a park for an insect larva. A caterpillar is one kind of larva. Other larvae may look like tiny worms. Look for insect eggs, too. They are likely to be round and very small. You will most likely find larvae and eggs on plants. Look on the undersides of leaves, for instance.

Ask an adult to punch airholes in a jar lid for you. Put the larva or eggs in the jar with the punched lid. Put in a few leaves from the plant where you found the larva or eggs, too. The leaves will be the insect's food.

Look at the larva or eggs through a magnifying glass or microscope. Describe or draw what you see. Then check it again every few days. See if you can keep the insect until it grows into an adult. When you have looked at it for a last time, let it go.

*Questions:*

How many legs does the larva have? How does it move? What can you see about its eyes and mouth? Does this kind of insect have a pupa stage? How long does the insect take to change into an adult? How is the adult different from the larva?

## Animal Muscle

*Materials needed:*

- animal muscle from uncooked steak, chicken or turkey leg, or lamb shank
- sharp knife
- magnifying glass or microscope
- glass slide or other clear surface
- paper and pencil or crayons

*Procedure:*

Meat is mostly muscle. *Working with an adult,* cut apart different kinds of meat and look at the muscle. Look for the membranes that divide the muscle into bundles. Look for other kinds of tissue, too. You will probably see bone and fat. You might see skin or blood vessels. Describe or draw what you see.

Spread a little of the muscle on a slide or other glass surface. Make it as thin as you can. Look at it with the magnifying glass or microscope. Describe or draw what you see.

*Questions:*

How is the muscle attached to the bone? What tissues do you see in the meat besides muscle? What job might each do? What does the muscle tissue itself look like? Can you see fibers in it? Can you see stripes in the fibers?

# Chronology

1632—Antoni van Leeuwenhoek is born on October 24, in Delft, Holland.

1638—Leeuwenhoek's father dies.

1640—Leeuwenhoek's mother remarries; Leeuwenhoek is sent to school in Warmond.

1648—Leeuwenhoek studies cloth-selling business in Amsterdam.

1654—Leeuwenhoek returns to Delft and opens cloth-selling shop. He marries Barbara de Mei and buys a house.

1656—Maria, the only one of Leeuwenhoek's children to grow to adulthood, is born.

1660—Leeuwenhoek becomes chamberlain for sheriffs of Delft.

1666—Barbara dies.

1668—Leeuwenhoek visits England and probably hears about Robert Hooke's *Micrographia.*

1669—Leeuwenhoek becomes surveyor.

1671—Leeuwenhoek begins making and using microscopes. He marries Cornelia Swalmius.

1673—Leeuwenhoek writes first letters to Royal Society of London.

1674—Leeuwenhoek sees "little animals" (protists) for first time.

1676—Leeuwenhoek discovers bacteria.

1677—Hooke shows "little animals" to Royal Society. Leeuwenhoek discovers sperm cells.

1680—Leeuwenhoek made Fellow of Royal Society.

1694—Cornelia dies.

1698—Leeuwenhoek visited by Peter the Great.

1711—Leeuwenhoek has twenty-six visitors in four days.

1716—Leeuwenhoek receives medal from University of Louvain (Belgium).

1723—Leeuwenhoek dies at Delft on August 26.

1739—Maria sets up monument over Leeuwenhoek's grave.

# Chapter Notes

## Chapter 1

1. William Montague, 1696, quoted in Clifford Dobell, *Antony van Leeuwenhoek and His "Little Animals"* (New York: Russell and Russell, 1958), p. 25.

2. Elizabeth Stuart, queen of Bohemia, quoted in Dobell, p. 29.

3. Dobell, p. 32.

4. Sir William Temple, quoted in Dobell, p. 40.

## Chapter 2

1. L. C. Palm, H.A.M. Snelders, eds., *Antoni van Leeuwenhoek 1632–1723* (Amsterdam: Editions Rodopi, 1982), p. 50.

2. Brian Ford, *Single Lens* (New York: Harper and Row, 1985), p. 28.

3. Brian Ford, *The Leeuwenhoek Legacy* (Bristol and London: Biopress and Farrand Press, 1991), p. 26.

4. Clifford Dobell, *Antony van Leeuwenhoek*

*and His "Little Animals"* (New York: Russell and Russell, 1958), p. 58.

5. Ibid.

6. Zacharias Conrad von Uffenbach, quoted in Ford, p. 49.

7. A. Schierbeek, *Measuring the Invisible World* (London and New York: Abelard-Schuman, 1959), p. 49.

**Chapter 3**

1. A. Schierbeek, *Measuring the Invisible World* (London and New York: Abelard-Schuman, 1959), p. 58.

2. Ibid.

3. Ibid., p. 59.

4. Ibid., p. 61.

5. Ibid.

6. Ibid.

7. Ibid., p. 65.

8. Brian Ford, *The Leeuwenhoek Legacy* (Bristol and London: Biopress and Farrand Press, 1991), p. 45.

9. Clifford Dobell, *Antony van Leeuwenhoek and His "Little Animals"* (New York: Russell and Russell, 1958), p. 83.

10. Ibid., p. 86.

11. Ibid., p. 200.

12. Samuel Hoole, trans., *The Select Works of Antony van Leeuwenhoek,* Vol. 1 (first printed 1798; reprint New York: Arno Press, 1977), p. v.

13. Ibid., p. 118.

14. Ibid.

15. Schierbeek, p. 73.

16. Dobell, p. 243.

17. Schierbeek, p. 78.

18. Rev. Jean Cornand de la Crose, quoted in Dobell, p. 62.

19. Schierbeek, p. 66.

## Chapter 4

1. Samuel Hoole, trans., *The Select Works of Antony van Leeuwenhoek* (first printed 1807; reprint New York: Arno Press, 1977), p. 162.

2. Ibid., p. 24.

3. Ibid., pp. 167–168.

4. Samuel Hoole, trans., *The Select Works of Antony van Leeuwenhoek,* Vol. 1 (first printed 1798; reprint New York: Arno Press, 1977), p. 39.

5. Ibid., p. 40.

6. Ibid., pp. 37–38.

7. Hoole, Vol. 2, pp. 22–23.

8. Ibid., p. 65.

9. Hoole, Vol. 1, p. 62.

10. Ibid., p. 138.

11. Hoole, Vol. 2, p. 191.

**Chapter 5**

1. Samuel Hoole, trans., *The Select Works of Antony van Leeuwenhoek,* Vol. 1 (first printed 1798; reprint New York: Arno Press, 1977), pp. 92–93.

2. Samuel Hoole, trans., *The Select Works of Antony van Leeuwenhoek*, Vol. 2 (first printed 1807; reprint New York: Arno Press, 1977), p. 216.

3. Ibid., p. 238.

4. A. Schierbeek, *Measuring the Invisible World* (London and New York: Abelard-Schuman, 1959), p. 111.

5. Hoole, Vol. 1, p. 231.

6. Schierbeek, p. 127.

7. *The Collected Letters of Antoni van Leeuwenhoek,* Vol. 4 (Amsterdam: Swets and Zeitlinger, 1952), p. 225.

8. Schierbeek, p. 124.

9. Hoole, Vol. 1, p. 260.

10. Ibid., p. 262.

11. Ibid., p. 274.

## Chapter 6

1. A. Schierbeek, *Measuring the Invisible World* (London and New York: Abelard-Schuman, 1959), p. 196.

2. Samuel Hoole, trans., *The Select Works of Antony van Leeuwenhoek*, Vol. 1 (first printed 1798; reprint New York: Arno Press, 1977), p. 19.

3. Ibid., p. 21.

4. Ibid., p. 23.

5. Ibid., p. 34.

6. Schierbeek, p. 87.

7. *The Collected Letters of Antoni van Leeuwenhoek*, Vol. 3 (Amsterdam: Swets and Zeitlinger, 1948), p. 35.

8. *The Collected Letters of Antoni van Leeuwenhoek*, Vol. 5 (Amsterdam: Swets and Zeitlinger, 1957), p. 209.

## Chapter 7

1. Clifford Dobell, *Antony van Leeuwenhoek and His "Little Animals"* (New York: Russell and Russell, 1958), p. 50.

2. Ibid.

3. Ibid., p. 56.

4. Ibid., p. 79.

5. Ibid., p. 78.

6. Zacharias Conrad von Uffenbach, quoted in Dobell, p. 69.

7. L. C. Palm, H.A.M. Snelders, eds., *Antoni van Leeuwenhoek 1632–1723* (Amsterdam: Editions Rodopi, 1982), p. 97.

8. Dobell, p. 75.

9. Ibid., p. 325.

10. Ibid., pp. 82–83.

11. Ibid., p. 87.

12. Ibid., p. 92.

13. Ibid., p. 99.

## Afterword

1. Clifford Dobell, *Antony van Leeuwenhoek and His "Little Animals"* (New York: Russell and Russell, 1958), p. 75.

2. Ibid., p. 76.

3. Ibid., p. 325.

4. Ibid., p. 74.

5. Ibid., p. 89.

6. Ibid., p. 74.

7. Samuel Hoole, trans., *The Select Works of Antony van Leeuwenhoek,* Vol. 2 (first printed 1807; reprint New York: Arno Press, 1977), pp. 274–275.

# Glossary

**artery**—A blood vessel that takes blood away from the heart to the rest of the body.

**bacteria**—The smallest living things. Each is a single cell with no nucleus. Some cause disease; others are helpful.

**capillary**—The smallest kind of blood vessel in the body. Capillaries connect the smallest arteries to the smallest veins, completing the circuit the blood makes through the body.

**cell**—The unit of which living things are made. Most cells can be seen only through a microscope. A membrane surrounds each cell and separates it from other cells.

**compound eye**—A large eye made up of many simple eyes. Many insects have compound eyes.

**compound microscope**—A microscope with more than one lens.

**concave**—Curving inward, like a bowl.

**convex**—Bulging or curving outward.

**egg cell**—The sex cell made by a female animal.

**fertilized egg**—The combination of an egg cell and a sperm cell. It divides and grows to become a new living thing.

**gall**—A swelling on a plant. It often is caused by an insect.

*Giardia*—A type of protist that can cause intestinal disease.

**larva**—The wormlike young of many insects; sometimes also called a maggot. A caterpillar is an example. Plural: **larvae.**

**lens**—A piece of transparent material, usually curved, that focuses (brings together) rays of light to form a clear image.

**louse**—A small insect that lives on the skin of people or animals and sucks blood. Plural: **lice.**

**microbe**—A living thing so small that it can be seen only with a microscope.

**microscope**—A device that uses one or more lenses to make objects look larger than they really are.

**nucleus**—A central part of most living cells. It controls the cell's activities.

**plaque**—A thick, white substance that forms on

teeth. It is made of food bits, saliva, and bacteria.

**protist**—A simple kind of living thing that is neither plant nor animal. Most protists can be seen only with a microscope. Unlike bacteria, protist cells have a nucleus.

**pupa**—The stage in the lives of some insects in which the insect changes from larva to adult form. A case usually protects the insect while it is a pupa.

**semen**—A thick fluid that comes from a male's sex organ during mating. It contains millions of sperm cells.

**simple eye**—A small eye of simple structure. The compound eye of an insect is made up of thousands of simple eyes.

**simple microscope**—A microscope that has only one lens.

**sperm cell**—The sex cell made by a male animal.

**spinneret**—The body organ, in most spiders and some insects, that makes a silky thread.

**tissue**—A group of cells that look alike and do the same job. Muscle and bone are examples.

**vein**—A blood vessel that carries blood from the body toward the heart.

**vorticella**—A protist, with a bell-shaped body and long tail, that attaches itself to water plants.

# Further Reading

Bleifeld, Maurice. *Experimenting with a Microscope*. New York: Franklin Watts Inc., 1988.

Canault, Nina. *Incredibly Small*. Englewood Cliffs, N.J.: Silver Burdett Press, 1993.

Loewer, Peter. *Pond Water Zoo: An Introduction to Microscopic Life*. New York: Simon & Schuster Children's, 1995.

Ozer, Steven. *Netherlands*. New York: Chelsea House Publishers, 1990.

Spangenburg, Ray and Diane K. Moser. *The History of Science from the Ancient Greeks to the Scientific Revolution*. New York: Facts on File, Inc., 1993.

——. *The History of Science in the Eighteenth Century*. New York: Facts on File, Inc., 1993.

Tomb, Howard. *Microaliens: Dazzling Journeys with an Electron Microscope*. New York: Farrar, Straus & Giroux, Inc., 1993.

# Index